## Credits

Rich Eames: Keyboards, Arranger, Recording Engineer
Tom Warrington: Electric Bass
Steve Houghton: Drums (demo tracks), Arranger
Andy Waterman: Recording Engineer (demo tracks)
Keith Blake: Mastering

## Special Thanks To

Sandy Feldstein
Ed Soph
Bob Breithaupt ... "The Art of the Drum Solo"
Joe Testa
My Students
All the Great Soloists

*Stream or download the audio content for this book.*
*To access, visit:* **alfred.com/redeem**
*Enter the following code:* 00-EL9602CD-664422

**alfred.com**

Copyright © 1996 by Alfred Music
All rights reserved.  Printed in USA.

ISBN-10: 0-7692-3470-4 (Book & Online Audio)
ISBN-13: 978-0-7692-3470-0 (Book & Online Audio)

Editor: Joe Testa
Photography: Roberto Santos
Art Design: Joseph Klucar

# CONTENTS

Internationally respected as a jazz drummer, percussionist, clinician and educator, Steve Houghton has shared both stage and studio with jazz and pop legends, including Joe Henderson, Arturo Sandoval, Rosemary Clooney, Scott Henderson, Melissa Manchester and Barbra Streisand. A Wisconsin native, Houghton attended the University of North Texas and received his first acclaim at the age of 20 as drummer with Woody Herman's Young Thunderbird Herd. After two years with the Herd, Houghton polished his reading skills in Dallas studios for four years and then moved to California, where he quickly established himself through his tenure with Toshiko Akiyoshi. In 1980, a last-minute call to substitute for Freddie Hubbard's drummer evolved into a two-year association. By the mid-'80s, Houghton, a busy Los Angeles studio musician, was writing, teaching at area universities and performing with symphony orchestras as a featured guest percussionist.

Houghton's recent recordings include *Windsong* (Shperc Records), *Steve Houghton* (Signature - Mesa Bluemoon) and *Remembrances* (with Dave Samuels - available from Warner Bros. Publications). He may also be heard on *The Music of Pat Metheny & Lyle Mays with Bob Curnow's L.A. Big Band* (MAMA Foundation) and *The Bob Florence Limited Edition.*

In addition to his recordings, Steve is also the author of more than 20 composite educational publications, including *The Drum Set Performer* (instructional book/CD play-along package), *The Drum Set Soloist* (instructional book/CD play-along package), *The Contemporary Rhythm Section* (text and video series), *Essential Styles* (book/CD play-along package) and his most recent collection, *The Percussion Recital Series* (a four-book/CD instructional and play-along series for timpani, keyboard percussion, multiple percussion and drum set).

Houghton is a member of the Percussive Arts Society board of directors and chairman of the International Association of Jazz Educators resource team. He endorses Pearl/Adams Percussion, Zildjian, Calato-Regal Tip and Remo products.

## PREFACE

Have you ever had to take a drum solo and found yourself scared to death? Often times drummers are called upon to solo and they are caught basically unprepared. I've found that many drummers don't <u>practice</u> soloing and for that reason they lack the confidence and the concept for soloing in a variety of settings. Soloing brings together three different aspects of drumming: technique, style and reading.

As this book will demonstrate, there are many solo formats and situations. Likewise, with each solo there are different requirements and different considerations.

This book will cover three basic solo formats; trading, playing over vamps and playing over kicks or figures. While these three are perhaps the most important, there are others. A few of them are:

1. form
2. harmonic rhythm
3. melody
4. open/free
5. transition solo - going from one style to another
6. transcriptions

While a drummer should have exposure to all these formats, the three that I've selected for the book will get you started in a good direction.

I hope this book will challenge you, inspire you and, most of all, let you create and improvise without the pressure of a live gig.

Have fun and good luck!

STEVE HOUGHTON

# THE ART OF THE DRUM SOLO

Any of us that have been dazzled by Buddy Rich, stunned by Dennis Chambers, or moved by Ed Blackwell, can appreciate the power and emotion created by the art of the drum solo. To list all the great drum soloists would be an exhaustive project, taking more pages than we have. However, a short overview of some of the outstanding drummers whose solos are a part of our lineage should be enlightening and helpful in studying the medium.

Even before the advent of the drum set around 1900, there were drummers, such as New Orleans bass drummer "Black Benny," that were famous for their soloing skill. It was in the early days of this century that the rudimental-oriented "ragtime" drum solo had its roots in Vaudeville, with drummers such as Jack Powell and "Traps the Boy Wonder" (Buddy Rich,) as well as with the early drum set players Buddy Gilmore and Tony Sbarbaro. Early Dixieland drummers "Baby" Dodds, Vic Berton and Zutty Singleton established themselves as fine ensemble players, as well as creative soloists. The Swing Era of the thirties and forties provided us with our first great drum soloists in players like Chuck Webb, Buddy Rich, Louie Bellson and Gene Krupa, who was and continues to be our most important force, bringing equal notoriety to the drummer to millions worldwide though his work with the famous Benny Goodman group. For the next twenty years, jazz was king and its most famous drum soloists such as Sid Catlett, Max Roach, Art Blakey, Philly Joe Jones, Roy Haynes, Elvin Jones and Tony Williams expanded the role and capability of the drummer to include playing drum solos as a melodic improviser over tune forms.

In the fifties and sixties, drum soloists again captured the imagination of listeners with Cozy Cole, Sandy Nelson, Ginger Baker, Ron Bushy and John Bonham, among others, achieving great commercial success with drum solo features on record. During the same time the free jazz movement spawned a number of creative drum soloists (Ed Blackwell, Rasheed Ali, Sonny Murray, Andrew Cyrille) whose expressiveness was a hallmark of style. Curiously, these efforts laid the foundation for the later virtuosi solo displays of Jack DeJohnette and Terry Bozzio.

As we enjoy Steve Gadd, Vinnie Colaiuta, Dave Weckl, "Smitty" Smith, Alex Acuna, Neal Peart, Peter Erskine, Trilock Gurtu, Steve Smith and the many other fine drum soloists today, we must all appreciate where these terrific ideas came from and how much wonderful music there is yet to discover.

# SOLO FORMATS

This book examines three different solo formats:

## 1. Trading (Tracks 1-11)

Trading is basically an exchange of ideas (rhythmic and melodic) between the melodic soloist and the drummer. Their exchange usually takes place in regular intervals throughout the tune. 2's, 4's, 8's and 12's are the most common length of phrases to be traded. However, one must practice trading in all styles at all tempos in order to be prepared for any solo situation.

In addition, certain tunes or song forms, (32 bar tune, 12 bar blues) set up accepted trading sequences, therefore, it is always important to know the form and length of the particular song so that the trading will make musical sense.

## 2. Vamps/Ostinatos (Tracks 12-20)

This solo format is very challenging, yet rewarding. This format utilizes some kind of rhythmic figure or feel that keeps repeating. This results in laying down a "pad" for the drummer to solo over. Again, this can take many forms stylistically and cover many different tempos. The key here is to develop the ability to not only play the rhythmic figure, but also play around the figure using all the soloistic elements discussed earlier. Since the format involves repetition, it is necessary to make the solo *build* musically, not just stay at the same intensity.

## 3. Kicks/Figures (Tracks 21-31)

This solo format is perhaps the newest solo situation. This setting utilizes a series of rhythmic kicks or figures that the drummer must not only catch, but also solo around. There are usually several different rhythmic hits which when played together create a longer musical phrase.

This format has a repetitive nature to it as well, but the manner in which the kicks are played makes this one of the more rewarding formats. Since the band has the job of playing the hits in time and in the same place, the soloist has the responsibility to solo in perfect time. Rushing, dragging, or loosing where the beat is makes it impossible to effectively play this solo format.

# NOTES FOR THE SOLOIST

Soloing is a skill that must be practiced regularly just like any of the other elements of drumming (technique, style and reading.) A drum solo can be a very unnerving experience for some drummers, as they may lack a broad overview of the music. The art of soloing demands that several musical concepts be solidly understood, not to mention having the proper technique to execute your ideas.

Understanding the following concepts will enable the soloist to feel more comfortable and musical in any soloistic setting.

## 1. Counting

Many inexperienced soloists get horribly lost when starting to take a solo. This counting problem becomes very apparent when "trading" with the band and not knowing when your solo is finished. It is a good idea to start counting out loud in the beginning, until it becomes second nature. In addition, a musician must develop a counting level which hears the big phrase and always knows where "one" is. This counting level will enable the soloist to "take it out" and play creatively over the bar line, always knowing where the phrase is.

## 2. Feeling 2 And 4

Not feeling beats 2 and 4 is a very common problem for the young soloist in that they lose where "one" is. It is important to try to keep the hi-hat going on beats 2 and 4 in jazz. This will, of course, help the drummer keep their place in the phrase and in the song. The hi-hat can serve as a crutch for the beginning soloist.

## 3. Stylistic Awareness

It is vital that the soloist know what note value ( o, ♩, ♩, ♪, ♪, ♫♫ ) the particular style is based on. This will provide the soloist with not only a broader view of the music but with actual soloistic material. For example, a medium swing tune is based on a triplet, therefore, it is a good idea to utilize triplets as part of the solo material. Understanding this will make the solo sound more authentic and in the style. Likewise, contrasting rhythms, such as sixteenth notes, can be used to create a kind of tension against the triplets.

## 4. Sticking Patterns

Often, soloists' ideas are limited by their sticking patterns. Quite simply, the more sticking patterns one knows, the more different ways around the drums are possible. In addition, speed can be addressed by utilizing effective sticking patterns.

## 5. Independence

Unfortunately, many drummers don't possess the independence to solo comfortably. This may be something as simple as keeping the hi-hat on 2 and 4 while soloing or as complex as soloing while your hi-hat plays clave and the bass drum plays a mambo pattern. Good independence makes for effortless, creative solos.

## 6. Melodic Awareness

Not being aware of a song's melody is a common oversight by young soloists. The drummer must be knowledgeable of not only the melody, but also the harmony of the tune. Melodic ideas can and should make their way into drum solos. Therefore, it is good to encourage the drummer to think and play melodically. A good method of practice is to play the melodies of jazz standards on the drums and memorize as many as possible.

## 7. Form

It is all too commonplace for drummers not to understand the form of a tune. The form of a tune is not only the roadmap, but also the skeleton of the tune. The drummer must understand the form, phrasing, harmonic rhythm, etc. to really participate effectively in the tune and solo inside of it.

## ABOUT THE DEMOS

This book/recording includes eight demonstration tracks (demos) as well as complete solo transcriptions. The purpose of the demos are to provide the listener with a sample approach to soloing in a particular situation/format. Obviously, soloing is a very individual process, but there are definite musical concepts that must be understood and utilized in order for the solo to really make musical sense. Dynamics, rhythmic quotation, contrast, metric modulation, interchanging styles, polyrhythms, displacement, augmentation, and motivic development, are just a few of the concepts that can be employed.

On the recording, the demo track always precedes the "open" track so the listener can get a better idea of the soloistic concept. A detailed solo transcription along with the form of the tune will provide the player with an inside look at melodic concepts and solo phrasing. These transcriptions are meant to be viewed only as a source of ideas and the player is encouraged to play part or all of the transcriptions. However, the player should strive to develop his/her own solo style.

In addition, there are short analyses of the solo techniques used in the demos to make it clear when, where and why certain ideas work effectively.

## ABOUT THE CHARTS

### Band Figures
The drum charts all reflect the form and the length of the tune, with appropriate repeats and endings. Where there are band figures in the arrangement they are notated above the staff.
Example:

### Drum Parts
When a specific drum pattern or part is needed, it will be notated as follows:

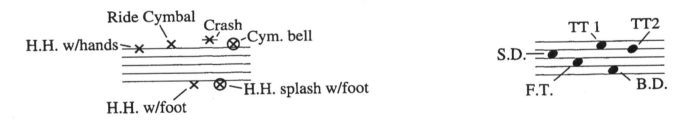

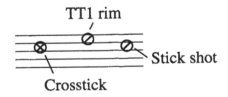

#### Crosstick
This refers to the left stick being layed across the snare drum with the fat end of the stick striking the rim thereby creating the characteristic wood block sound.

#### Stick Shot
This technique developed in the 1930's, places the tip of the left stick on the snare head and then striking it (the left stick) with the right stick.

**Form**

Each chart, within the trading section, contains a form summary. This can be found at the bottom of the chart. The form summary gives the player the complete roadmap of the piece including how many choruses or complete times through the pieces. A chorus will be notated by x. Example: 1 chorus = 1 time through = 1x.

**"Based On" Groove**

Finally, in the Vamps/Ostinatos and Kicks/Figures sections, each "open" track has a rhythm or groove it is based on. These grooves will be notated at the start of each track.

## SLOW BLUES

This track is based on a basic 12 bar blues form, with the drums trading 2's after two full choruses. The piano will take the first 2 bar solo and then it's the drummer's turn. One approach is to play off of what the previous soloist played and continue their melodic or rhythmic idea on the drums. Triplet rhythms work well at this tempo and in this style, however, contrasting sixteenth note double-time feel rhythms provide nice contrast. Try and make the tradeoffs very smooth and listen for the ending. By the way, the last chorus doesn't have "snaps" on 2 and 4, so really work to get the inner clock happening.

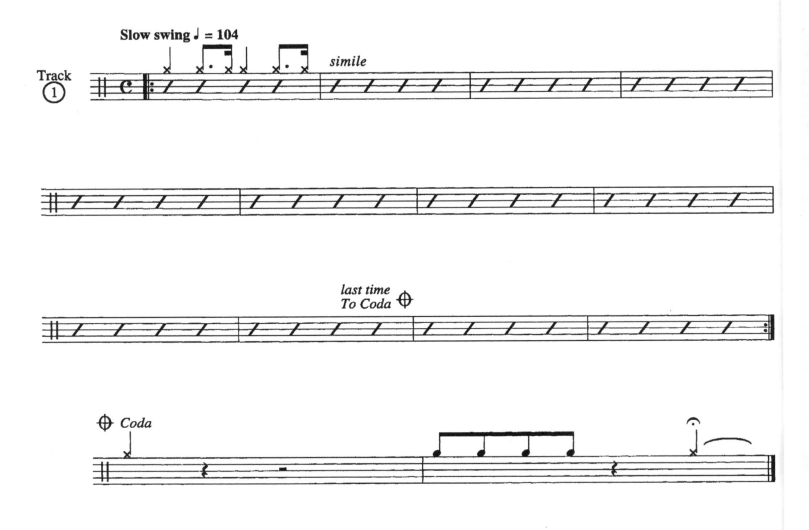

FORM:     Play through 2x's, then trade 2's with the band, the band taking the first 2.
              3x w/click.
              1x wo/click.
              Last 2x's, play time and take coda.

## MEDIUM BLUES

This 12 bar blues should be propelled by a driving quarter note ride cymbal beat. Again, listen and react to the melodic and rhythmic quotes from the piano. You will be thinking 4 bar phrases this time, so think longer ideas. There are rhythmic "sendoffs" at the end of the piano solos that should be utilized. Example:

There are no clicks the last chorus so be sure and keep counting. The ending is a very traditional jazz ending, so learn it and memorize it!!

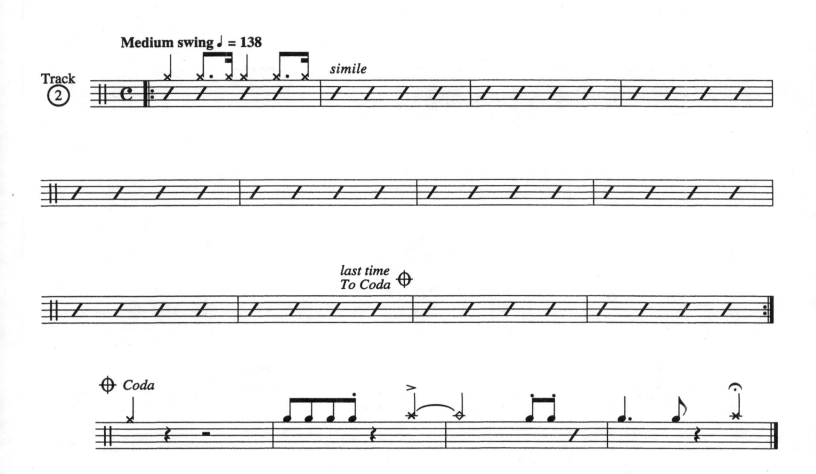

FORM:   Play though 2x's then trade 4's.
Band plays first 4.
7x w/click.
1x wo/click.
Play time the last 2 choruses and take coda last x.

## RHYTHM CHANGES DEMO

This tune is based on "Rhythm" changes which is the jazz vocabulary for the chord changes to a standard jazz tune, "I Got Rhythm." The form of this 32 bar tune is AABA. The feel is a driving quarter note feel, with the drums trading 8's. The piano takes the first solo.

In the first solo, I tried to make it a time oriented solo utilizing the ride cymbal and not using toms. I also utilized different melodic combinations on the set. For example, the first 8 features the snare and ride cymbal as a unison voice creating a line with the hi-hat. The second 8 worked off the rhythm played by the piano at the end of his solo. The rhythm he played was    with a straight, not swing, feel. I choose to start my next solo the same way with rim shots. The last part of my solo included a rhythm which the piano immediately picks up on. A similar exchange takes place at the end of the piano players solo. Good trading involves a constant dialogue between soloists.

## RHYTHM CHANGES

It is important to understand the form of this tune, which is AABA. When trading 8's with the piano, listen to the endings of the piano solos for possible solo ideas (see demo notes.) Triplet material, as well as "swing" eighth note material, will work well. There are no clicks on the last solo chorus, so internalize the time. Watch and listen for the short ending.

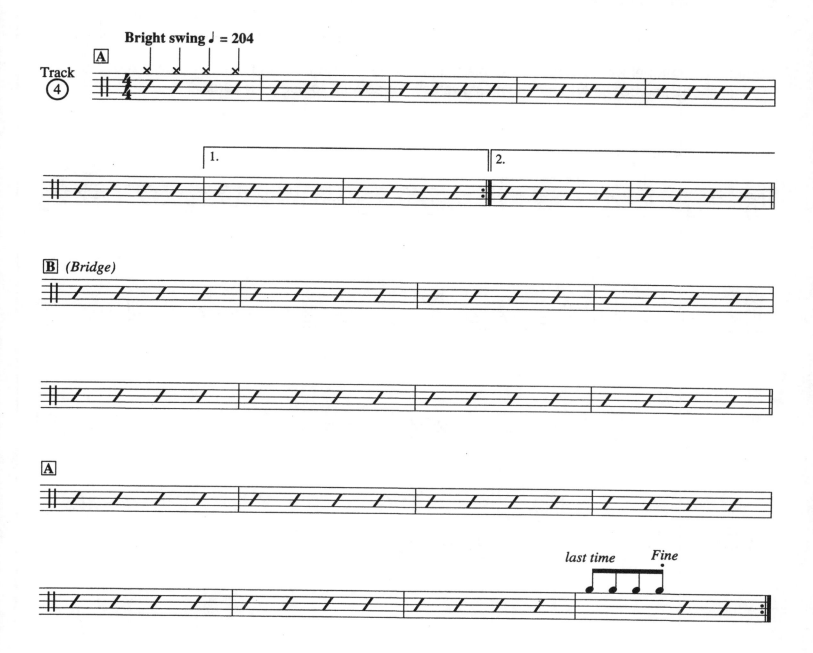

FORM:    32 bar tune - AABA.
Play time for 1 chorus, then trade 8's.
Band takes first 8.
2x w/click.
1x wo/click.
Play time on the last chorus and play the ending in bar 32.

## 3/4 SWING

When playing in "3" there are many inflections that can take place. Be sure to listen to the bass player to hear whether the feel is  or . This will determine many of the cymbal as well as the bass drum/snare drum comping patterns. When playing in three, superimposing four over the top can be very effective. Example:

Triplet solo material works very well at this tempo as does swing eighth notes. The click drops out on the last chorus, so be ready! The ending slows down gradually so use your ears.

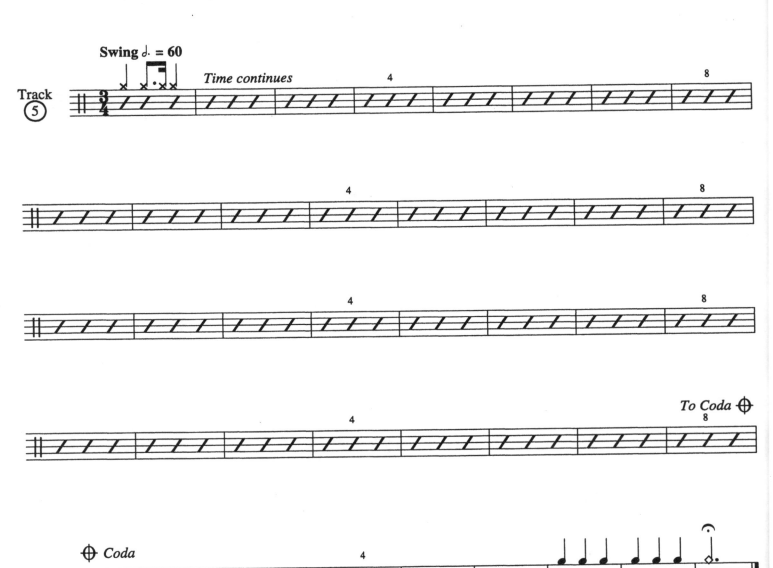

FORM:  Play time 1st time through then trade 8's.
Band plays first 8.
3x w/click.
1x wo/ click.
Play through last time and take Coda.

14

## UP TEMPO BLUES

This blues is a little too fast for the triplets, therefore, the solo material can be more eighth note oriented. At this tempo, the drummer usually takes a whole chorus (12 bars), so it is vital that the soloist know the form of the tune and the top of the chorus. Be sure to listen to the last few bars of the piano solo for connecting ideas. One approach is to play a very simple melodic rhythm on the drum stating the time very clearly. Example:

Phrase wise, the drummer may think 4, 8, or 12 bar phrases. The ending is a very traditional jazz ending. NOTE: Make sure each chorus builds in intensity, so that your last solo chorus is really exciting and leads the band into the "out chorus."

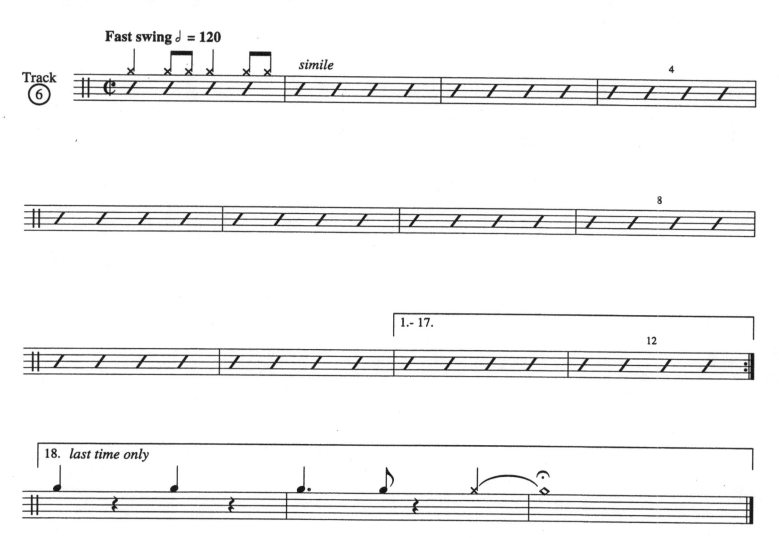

FORM:    Play tune through 2 times, then trade choruses (12 bars) with the band.
Drums will trade 7x's or 14 choruses.
Play time on the last two "out" choruses and take last ending.

## 32-BAR TUNE

This track is an example of a tune that utilizes decreasing 8's, 4's 2's and 1's. This solo format was made popular by the late Bill Evans. This format builds energy into the tune almost automatically, as the solos get shorter and shorter. The melodic soloist and the drummer have to really be locked in on the sequence, especially as the trading gets quicker. Again, listening to what was played before you is a must, if the melodic flow is to continue, especially when it gets down to 2's and 1's. Obviously, the form and length of the tune must be second nature for the drummer to fully interact with the other soloists.

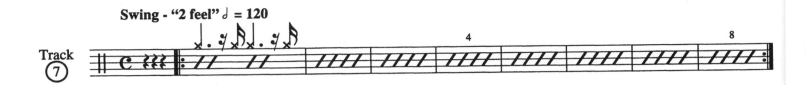

FORM:  Play entire tune then start trading.
2x = 8's.
1x = 4's.
24 bars = 2's.
8 bars = 1's.
Play time last x through and take Coda.

## FAST MODAL

These kinds of tunes generally have two things that one can count on. First of all, the form is usually AABA, with the length of the tune being 32 bars. The other is some kind of rhythmic motif that keeps coming up in the melody or the solo. Example:

The trading sequence is 8's. This tempo demands an eighth note concept for soloing. Often times, soloists seem limited by their sticking patterns and orchestration ideas, so take the time to work out a variety of eighth note sticking patterns for the hands and feet. Simplicity is something that shouldn't be overlooked at this tempo. Always try to think melodically, even at this tempo.

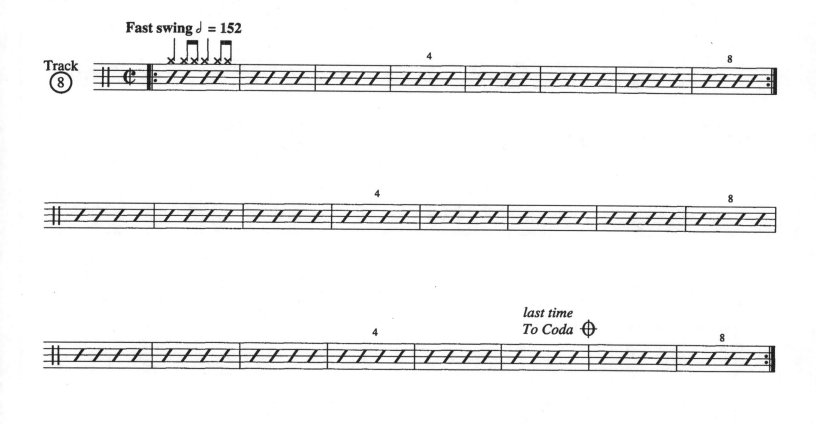

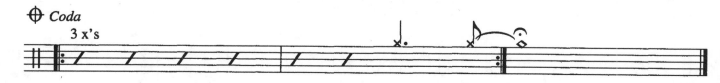

FORM:     Play time first time through then trade 8's.
          Band take first 8.
          4x w/click on 1's.
          1x w/o click.
          Play time last x through and take the Coda.

## MEDIUM LATIN DEMO

This bossa nova is 40 bars long and the form is ABA, with the bridge being 8 bars long. Trading 4's are utilized again, with the first drum solo being time oriented. It is almost like a continuation of the groove, with some subtle embellishments at the end of the phrase. In the Latin feel, the crosstick patterns are very prominent, therefore, it is a nice idea to have a solo on crosstick variations. Continuity, flow and smoothness are very important in the tune, so the solos must be dynamically in balance with what came before it. The second chorus of trading employs a rhythmic dialogue between the piano and the drums. As the tune progresses, the solos may become more complex and adventuresome.

* The five "flams" included in these 2 bars are accomplished by one hand in the following manner: The bead of the left stick is placed on the snare drum in order to execute the cross stick, which is the principle note of the flam. However, just before that cross stick, the left stick hits the rim of tom tom 1, which serves as the grace note of the flam. The technique is credited to John Guerin.

## MEDIUM LATIN

This bossa nova is a 40 bar tune with an ABA form, with the drums trading 4's in the Latin style. Many of the techniques discussed earlier apply in this style as well. The most important thing to consider is not interrupting the groove/feel with your solo. Try and make it blend into the music. Know the melodic soloist will pass you some strong rhythmic ideas to work with. One approach to soloing in Latin would be to let the bass drum continue an ostinato:

and solo over it. The other approach is to utilize the bass drum as another solo voice.

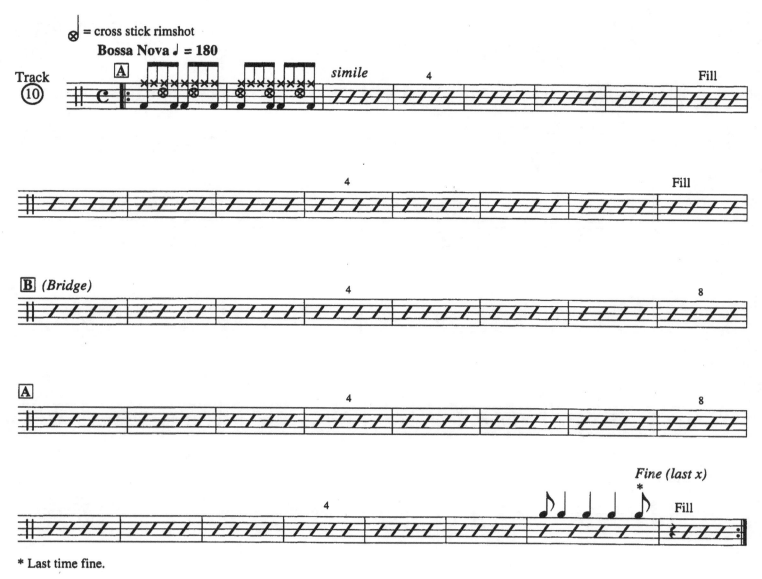

\* Last time fine.

FORM:    40 bar tune - ABA.
                   Play time for 1 chorus then trade 4's.
                   Band take first 4.
                   2x w/click.
                   1x w/o click.
                   Play down to Fine.

## BRIGHT SAMBA

This bright samba is a 16 bar tune, with a 16 bar intro. All the comments made for Medium Latin hold true here. In this tune however, the band trades 8's with the drums so the phrases can be extended. Try to solo over the bar line using 3 against 4 and other polyrhythms. To solo effectively in this style, one must understand Brazilian music. In this style, the surdo (big drum) hits on beat three. If understood, this can be worked into the solo. In addition, this samba is based on a rhythm called Partido Alto. Example:

FORM: Play intro...then play tune 2x's through...then trade 8's.
    6x - trading 8's.
    Play through tune...take repeat and then go to the Coda.

*This page has been left blank to facilitate page turns.*

## ECM DEMO

ECM is a record label that features primarily straight eighth note jazz music. This music tends to be very cymbal oriented, along with somewhat repetitive bass lines. The style is very improvisatory, so backbeats aren't needed. The solo format shown here is a repetitive vamp, rhythm or groove. The solo section starts with the drums embellishing on the original groove, first playing variations on the cymbal groove. Next, the drums are brought into the mix very sparsely. Eventually, tension is created by utilizing over the bar line, phrasing and polyrhythms. This solo format is wide open, where almost anything will work. Stylistic contrast can be used effectively by playing triplet ideas over a straight eighth note groove.

## ECM VAMP

This type of solo format is a vamp and can be found in the music of Pat Metheny. Many people refer to this style of music as E.C.M. music. The concept here is to state the groove and then start to embellish on it, starting simple and getting more complex (see demo). Utilizing triplet rhythms against an eighth note groove will add excitement, as well as tension. Going over the bar line with the phrasing will create a swirling effect. Superimposing different feels on top of the vamp will take the solo to another level.

Track ⑬

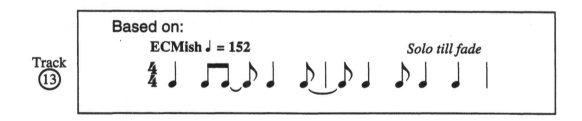

## JAZZ LATIN VAMP

This track features an ostinato pattern based on a piano comping rhythm. The drums have a lot of freedom in that they may approach it in at least three different ways. First of all, the drums can basically let the figure be played by the band and solo in the holes. Second, the drummer may play the figure and start to embellish on it. Finally, the drums may solo right through the figure, occasionally catching it, so everyone keeps their place. In this tempo, other styles such as half-time swing, uptempo swing and half-time rock all seem to work, so experiment.

## SALSA VAMP

The Salsa vamp represents a very common situation in Latin music where the rhythm section grooves and the drums or percussion (timbales, congas) solo over it. The soloist should listen to the bass line to get a feel for the 2 bar phrase. Rhythmically it is wide open, meaning the drums can use any rhythmic material in the solo. To become better at soloing in this style, it is a good idea to listen to timbale and conga players.

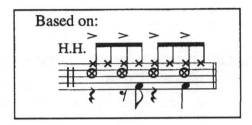

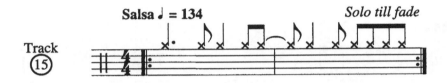

## VAMP IN "5"

This track has a Brazilian flavor to it, so try and make use of those elements (surdo sound, partido alto, samba bass drum, etc.). The figure may be caught each time, using it as a "lift off" to the solo. Another approach would be to solo through the kick. Since the track is solid and complete, it works well to just play a samba groove with simple embellishments.

Above all, make it feel good....even in "5." Note that eighth, sixteenth and triplet solo material all work in this vamp.

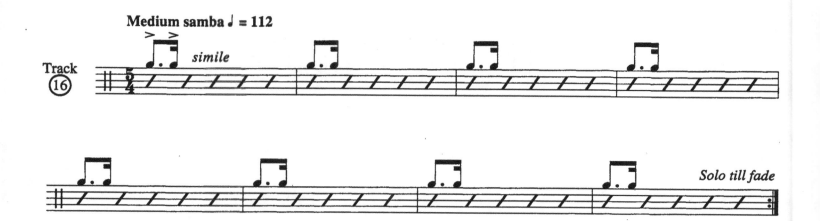

## VAMP IN "7"

This track has a couple of comping/ostinato elements to be aware of. The bass line is very important to the groove and will provide solo ideas. In addition, the piano comping rhythm provides another counter rhythm to play with. The rhythmic hit in the second bar of the vamp really makes for some interesting possibilities. For example, that rhythmic motif can be reintroduced at the beginning of the first bar and when played several times in a row offers some interesting results. Finally, two groups of 7 eighth notes equals one bar of seven. When phrasing in this fashion, it really gets interesting. Good luck.

Example:

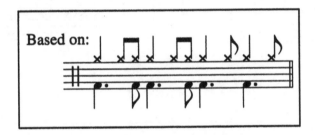

*Solo till fade*

27

## FUSION SAMBA DEMO

This track is based on a samba feel with the agogo bells playing a repetitive rhythm in the background. Example:

Agogo rhythm:

When starting to solo over the vamp, I just locked in on the groove with sixteenths on the hi-hat. The bass drum makes its way into the mix, then drums, sparsely at first with short little bursts. Eventually, a samba groove is created while soloing over the top.

Note: ⊗ = cym. bell or dome

## FUSION SAMBA VAMP

As mentioned in the demo notes, this track is based on a samba feel. As always, the drums have many ways to approach this track, the first being steady sixteenths, on hi-hat and add drums when comfortable. Another basic approach is to take the rhythmic motif and really work out on it, re-orchestrate and re-position it within the bar. As with most of the vamps, the feel should never be lost. It is sometimes a good idea to conceptualize your filling and soloing by simply playing "time" all over the kit.

Based on:

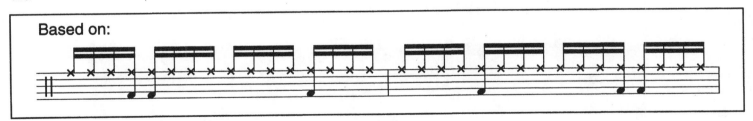

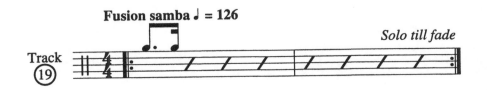

## MONTUNO VAMP

On this track, the soloist must immediately become aware of the mambo/songo groove set up by the bass. The piano part contains some strong solo material. Phrase-wise, this vamp could either be 4-2 bar phrases or 2-4 bar phrases. It is amazing how different the two sound. Implying the 6/8 feel over this track will really give it some authenticity, as well as looseness. The more playing over the bar line the better. Watch for the rhythm at the end of the vamp, eventually utilizing it in the solo phrasing. This vamp is based on a songo groove for the drums.

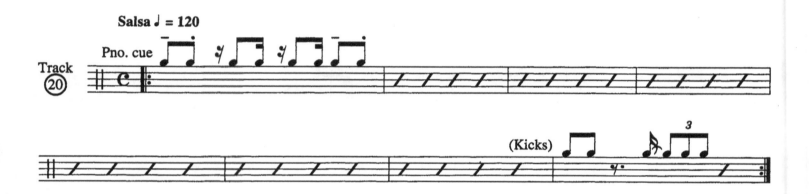

## HIP HOP W/KICKS

This track, although more of a contemporary rock or pop groove, has jazz elements in it as well. The kicks all must be interpreted with a swing feel and the band figure at the end of the phrase is actual triplets. One solo approach is to incorporate the kicks into your groove (BD), so you catch it automatically. Your solo material can again be eighths (swing and straight), triplets and sixteenths. In addition, odd groups might be experimented with. For example, eighth note triplets, accented every fourth note, create an interesting polyrhythm:

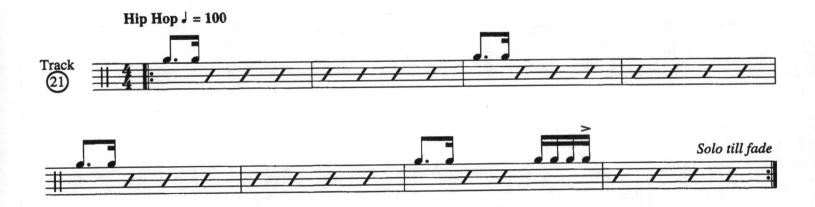

## SONGO DEMO

This solo format features playing over kicks that form an eight bar phrase and is based on a songo groove. The solo starts by playing the groove and catching the figures, especially in bars 4 and 8. Again, I choose to bring the drums in sparsely, and as the track builds, the ideas become longer and more complex. The triplet ideas work well for contrast in the straight eighth feel, suggesting the 6/8 Latin feel over the top of everything. When playing with kicks, one can either lay for the kicks and catch them or solo right through them.

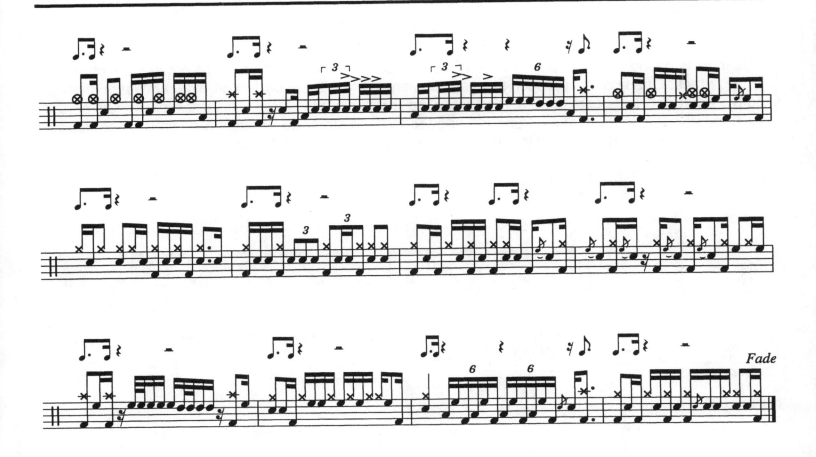

## SONGO W/KICKS

The ideas mentioned on the demo notes are important, such as understanding and being comfortable with the basic songo groove. A good exercise would be to keep the bass drum ostinato going and slowly build good independence with your hands against the ostinato. This is mandatory for a good feeling solo. Initially, ignore the kicks, but when comfortable, lay for the kicks and build the solo off of them. The relationship of 4/4 to 6/8 can't be stressed enough. In other words, use triplet ideas for a more authentic feel.

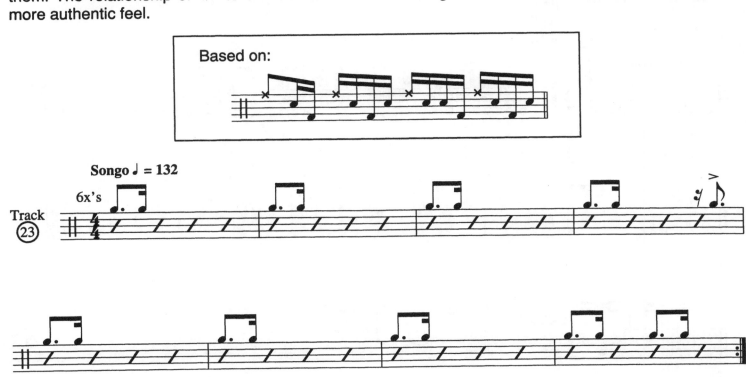

## $\frac{3}{4}$ FUSION DEMO

This track is based on a half-time groove in "3," that sets up a kick section which creates an interesting 8 bar phrase. One way to approach this very challenging feel is to play the groove and watch the kicks go by. When this feels comfortable, then start catching (hitting) the kicks. This track leaves lots of room for creativity. Playing 4 against 3 and utilizing the kicks to start odd phrases are two devices used on this demo. Eighth, sixteenth and triplet solo material all seem to work on the track.

Note: See page 36 for Based On.

# ¾ FUSION W/KICKS

As mentioned in the demo notes, the groove is of utmost importance in this track. Understand that effective solo sections can be achieved by tastefully embellishing the groove. When learning where the kicks fall, one might keep time on the ride cymbal ( ♩ ♩ ♩ ) while catching the hits on the snare. Really, the only way to solo with abandon is to memorize the kick sequence. Use some of the kicks to start a new phrase, even though it might fall in an awkward part of the bar. Have fun!!

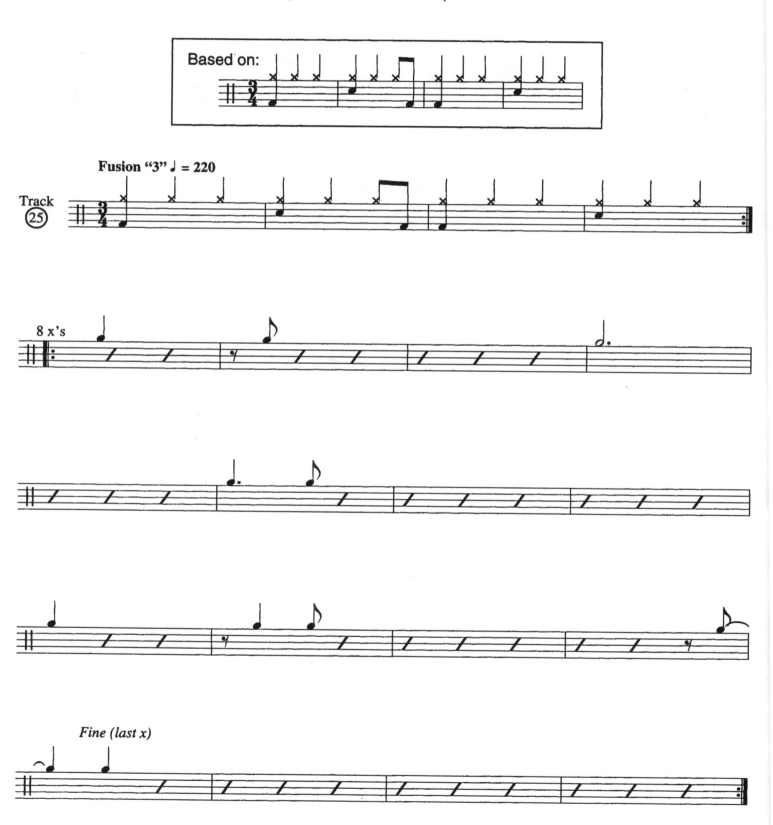

*This page has been left blank to facilitate page turns.*

## "WEATHER REPORT" FUSION DEMO

This track opens with a 4 bar intro that leads into a sixteen bar kick section that keeps repeating (8x's). I started this solo by playing the kicks on the bass drum while keeping a constant groove going with crosstick and ride cymbal. The second time through I added some backbeats on the snare. Third time through, some fills leading in and out of the kicks were needed. As the solo built, I played right through the kicks and resolved my phrases at odd times. The counting level mentioned earlier is important here in order to get the player to solo over the bar line and in long phrases.

Note: See page 40 for Based On.

## "WEATHER REPORT" FUSION W/KICKS

Once again, memorizing the kick sequence will enable the soloist to solo freely and inventively. When learning the track, keep a simple groove going to become comfortable with the track. Solo material can consist of eighth note ideas, but triplet ideas work very well at this tempo. Sixteenth notes will sound very exciting, so make sure that a variety of sticking patterns are learned. These kicks lay so well, the filling should really create a smooth intensity. Work to make every chorus a little more interesting. Implying a swing-shuffle feel over the bar line makes for a nice idea.

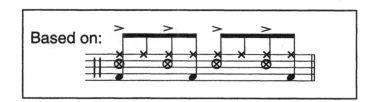

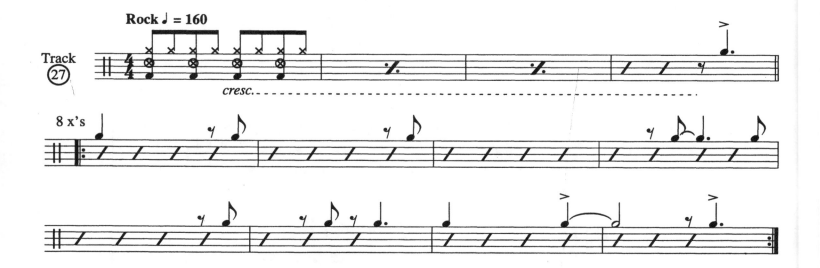

## "CHICK" FUSION W/KICKS

This track is reminiscent of something Chick Corea might play. After a four bar intro, a very syncopated kick section follows, creating an interesting five bar phrase. The trick is to incorporate the kicks into the drum part. The need here is to play a groove, catch the kicks and solo when feasible. In the third and fourth bar of the actual melody, there is a nice rhythmic motif that could be extended to a solo idea. The space left between kicks should eventually be utilized for fills. Also, play the kick in the last bar of the vamp.

Based on:

## FUSION SWING DEMO

Initially, I tried to create a very loose feel utilizing rolls, cymbal burst, etc., trying not to make the time too obvious. After the opening section, there are many kicks/figures to keep track of. I tried to take advantage of repetitive quarter notes or dotted quarter sections to create over the bar line phrases. Again, the figures can be played exactly, or played around with. The 32 bar intro is simply playing around this figure ( ♩. ♪♩ ). The kick section (tune) starts after that.

Note: See page 44 for Based On.

## FUSION SWING W/KICKS

When learning to play with this track, it is important to be able to play the up tempo swing feel. If the hi-hat is needed, use it. Eventually, you will want to achieve a looser, freer feel. In the kick section, start out by playing time on the ride cymbal and catching the kicks underneath it. Try using both snare drum and bass drum. Gradually, add some easy setups to some of the kicks. Again, the notes that repeat themselves are a good place to start overlapping ideas. (1st ending).

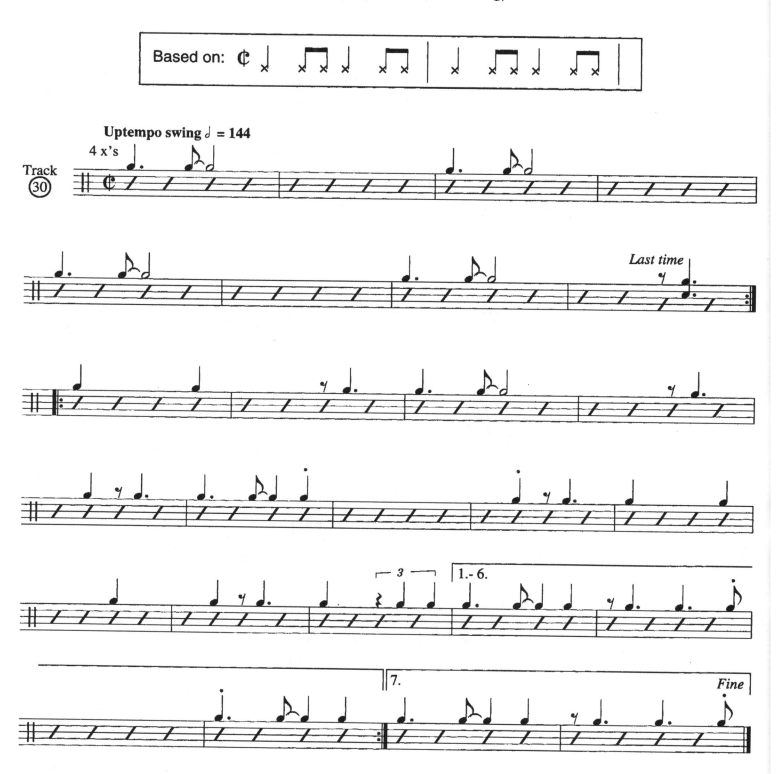

## MAMBO W/KICKS

The first part of this track is based on a mambo groove. When the kicks come in, the same groove can be played, while learning the hits. A songo groove will also work well. As with another Latin track, the 6/8 feel is implied or actually used with great success. Notice that there is a triplet figure used in the hit section. Don't be afraid to stretch your phrasing between the hits to give it that Latin flavor.

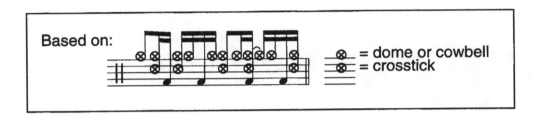

# THE DRUMMER'S GUIDE TO READING DRUM CHARTS

(VH0177)

The purpose of this video is to provide the drummer with a strong, overall concept for reading drumset charts. A detailed approach is used discussing musical definitions, stylizes reading, set-up techniques, sight-reading concepts, ensemble playing skills, and most important, chart analysis. In this analysis, a variety of charts are discussed and demonstrated, preparing the drummer to deal with reading in any musical situation. Hands on tips are supplied to help the drummer know what to do in "the heat of battle."

An extensive collection of twenty-two actual charts are used to demonstrate various problems and trouble spots when reading drum charts. The collection covers almost every reading situation and format the drummer might encounter.

"The Drummer's Guide to Reading Drum Charts is a vital asset to drummers of all ages and levels. If you're serious about drumming then you should be serious about this video."

— Gregg Bissonette

"The most clear-cut and practical approach to chart reading that exists today within the video medium."

— Ed Shaughnessy

"...an excellent primer course for drummers who want to prepare themselves for the experience of confronting a piece of music in any situation...an asset for any course of study."

— Peter Erskine

"Steve's video is a must for any drummer who is looking for a practical and musical approach to chart reading and interpretation."

— Ed Soph

"Steve is a master teacher! He breaks down chart reading to the essential building blocks and helps you construct a very coherent whole concept. Well done!"

— Steve Smith

"Any drummer who wants to know how to read drum charts should have this video. Great source material for teachers as well."

— Dave Garibaldi